Collins
My First book of
World Flags

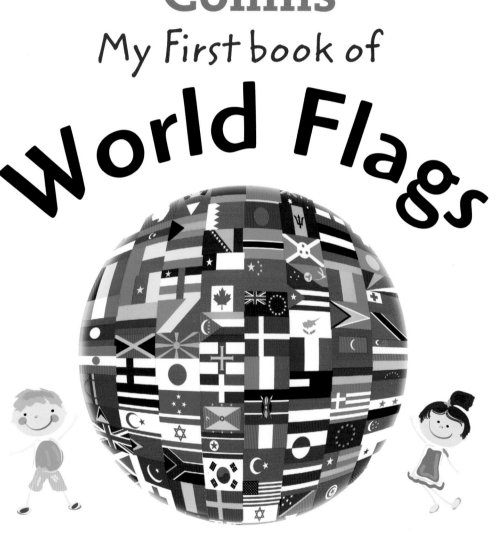

Collins My First Book of World Flags

Collins
An imprint of HarperCollins Publishers
77-85 Fulham Palace Road
London W6 8JB

© HarperCollins Publishers 2011
Maps © Collins Bartholomew Ltd 2011

First published 2011

ISBN 978-0-00-746046-5
ISBN 978-0-00-791026-7

Imp 001

British Library Cataloguing in Publication Data
A catalogue record for this book is available from the British Library.

Printed and bound in Singapore

All mapping in this atlas is generated from Collins Bartholomew digital databases.
Collins Bartholomew, the UK's leading independent geographical information supplier, can provide
a digital, custom, and premium mapping service to a variety of markets. For further information:
Tel: +44 (0) 141 306 3752
e-mail: collinsbartholomew@harpercollins.co.uk

Visit our websites at:
www.harpercollins.co.uk
www.collinsbartholomew.com
www.collinsmaps.com

Contents

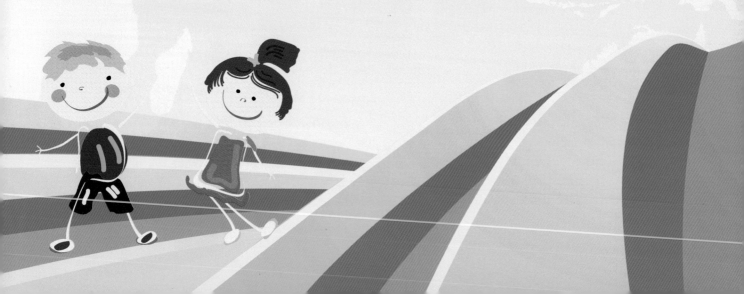

Flags are usually associated with countries, nations and international organizations. Flags are everywhere. They are used in football, racing, industry, schools, by explorers and armies. Flags come in all shapes, sizes and colours.

Europe

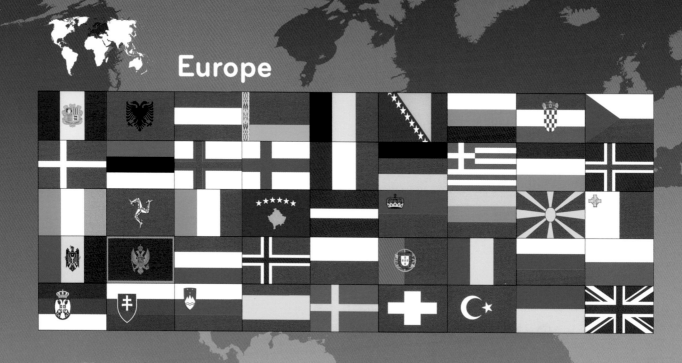

Africa

Asia

North America

South America

Oceania

Europe

France

Andorra

Monaco

Spain

Portugal

Bullfight
Madrid, Spain

Capital cities

Andorra	Andorra la Vella
France	Paris
Monaco	Monaco-Ville
Portugal	Lisbon
Spain	Madrid

Europe

Faroe Islands (Denmark)

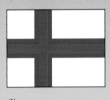

Iceland

Isle of Man (UK)

United Kingdom

Ireland

Jersey (UK)

Guernsey (UK)

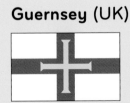

Capital cities

Faroe Islands (Denmark)	Tórshavn
Guernsey (UK)	St Peter Port
Iceland	Reykjavík
Ireland	Dublin
Isle of Man (UK)	Douglas
Jersey (UK)	St Helier
United Kingdom	London

Geyser eruption, Iceland

Europe

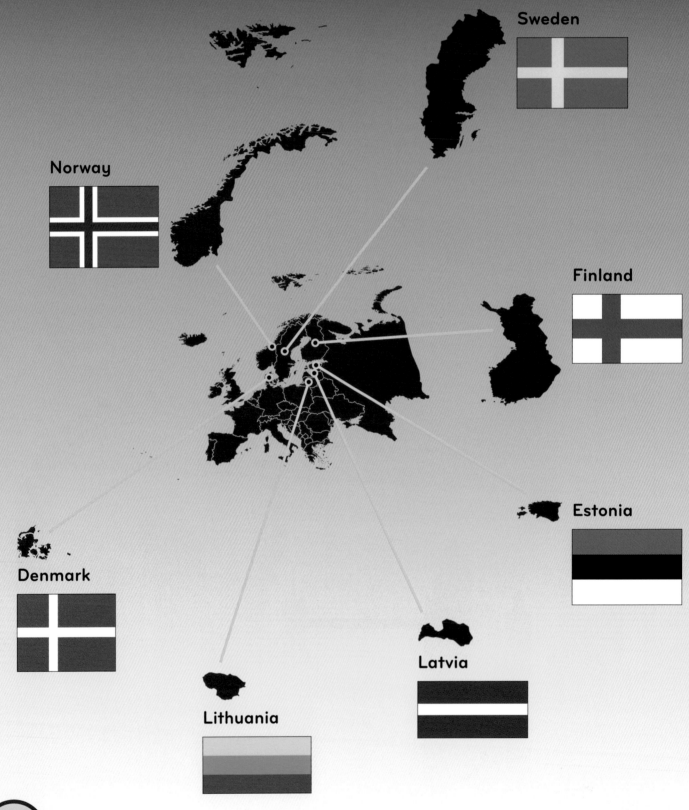

Sweden

Norway

Finland

Denmark

Estonia

Lithuania

Latvia

Capital cities

Denmark	Copenhagen
Estonia	Tallinn
Finland	Helsinki
Latvia	Rīga
Lithuania	Vilnius
Norway	Oslo
Sweden	Stockholm

Reindeer, Sweden

Europe

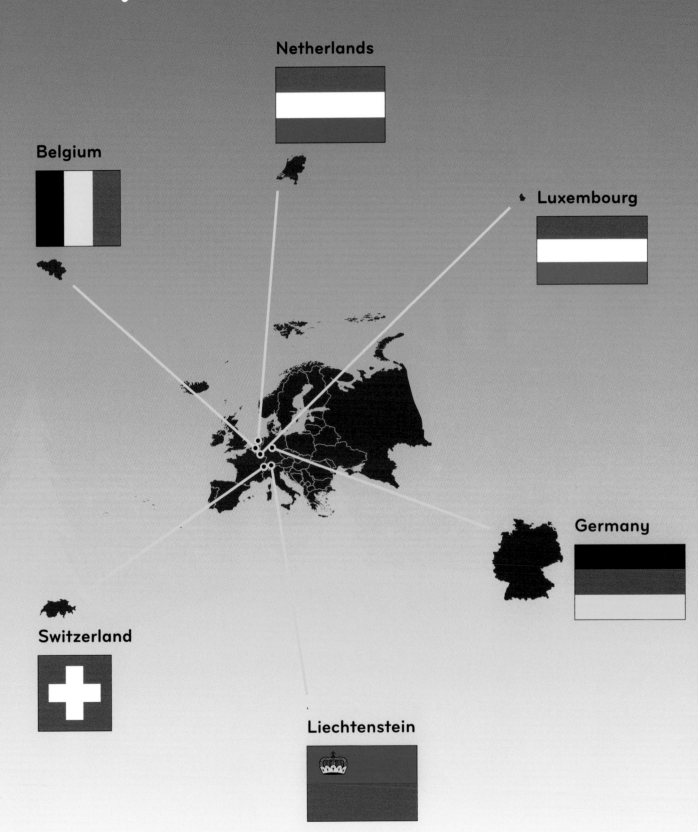

Netherlands

Belgium

Luxembourg

Germany

Switzerland

Liechtenstein

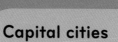

The river Rhine in Koblenz, Germany

Europe

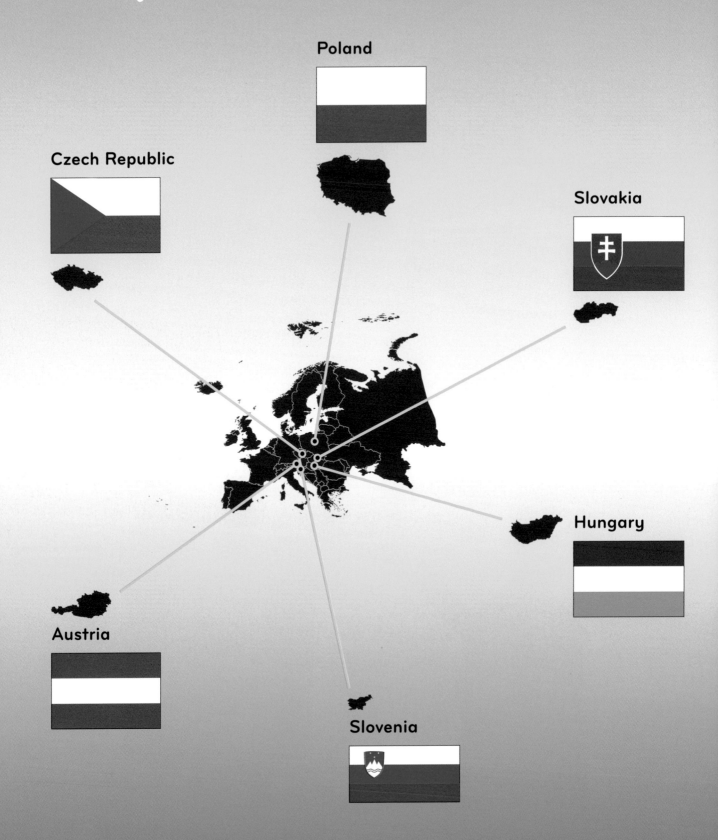

Poland

Czech Republic

Slovakia

Hungary

Austria

Slovenia

Capital cities

Austria	Vienna
Czech Republic	Prague
Hungary	Budapest
Poland	Warsaw
Slovakia	Bratislava
Slovenia	Ljubljana

Church of Our Lady,
Prague, Czech Republic

Europe

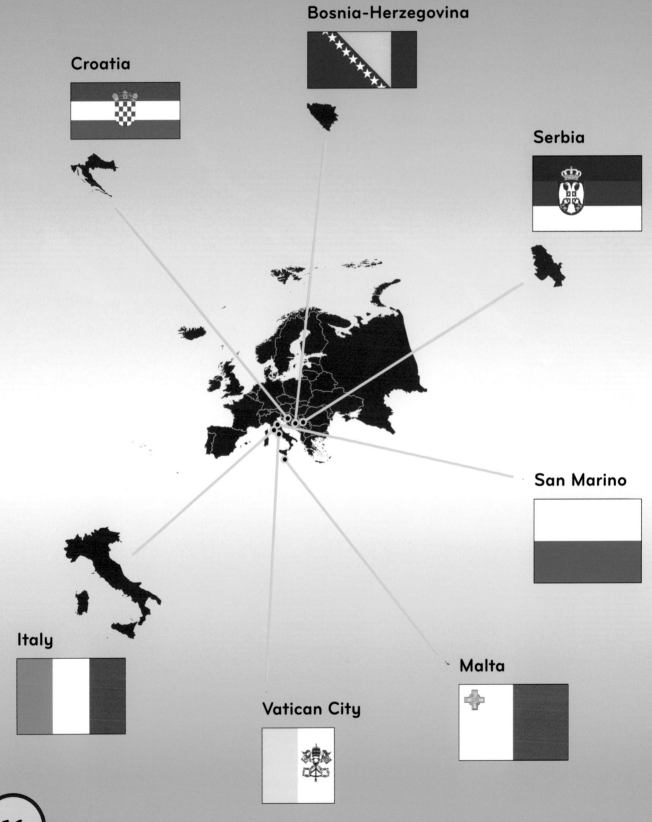

Croatia

Bosnia-Herzegovina

Serbia

San Marino

Italy

Vatican City

Malta

Capital cities

Bosnia-Herzegovina	Sarajevo
Croatia	Zagreb
Italy	Rome
Malta	Valletta
San Marino	San Marino
Serbia	Belgrade
Vatican City	Vatican City

Florence, Italy

Europe

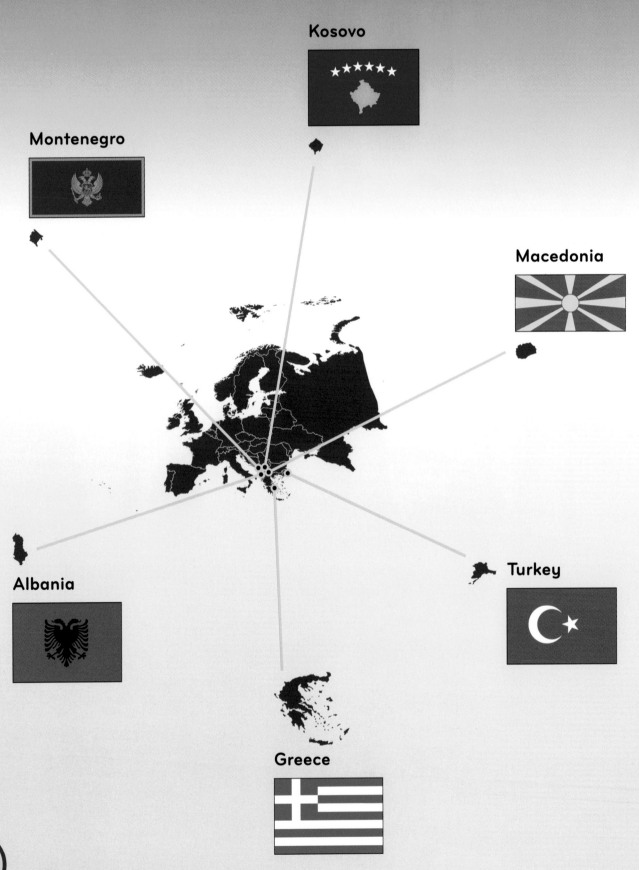

Kosovo

Montenegro

Macedonia

Albania

Turkey

Greece

Fishing boats in harbour,
Greece

Capital cities

Albania	Tirana
Greece	Athens
Kosovo	Pristina
Macedonia	Skopje
Montenegro	Podgorica
Turkey	Ankara

Europe

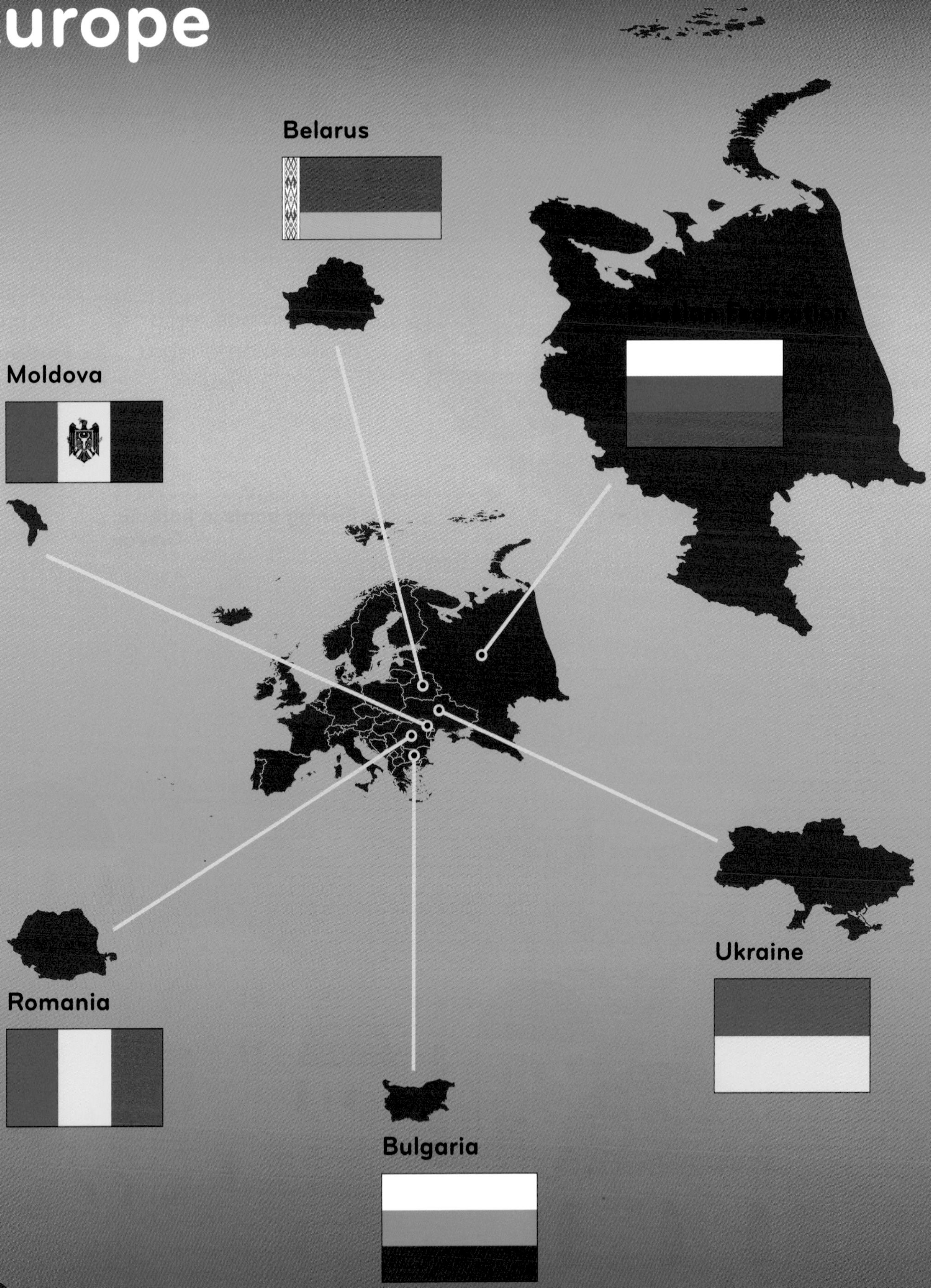

Belarus

Moldova

Russian Federation

Ukraine

Romania

Bulgaria

Cathedral in St Petersburg,
Russian Federation

Capital cities

Belarus	Minsk
Bulgaria	Sofia
Moldova	Chișinău
Romania	Bucharest
Russian Federation	Moscow
Ukraine	Kiev

Africa

Moroccan spices,
Marrakech, Morocco

Capital cities

Algeria	**Algiers**
Cape Verde	**Praia**
Egypt	**Cairo**
Libya	**Tripoli**
Mauritania	**Nouakchott**
Morocco	**Rabat**
Tunisia	**Tunis**
Western Sahara	**Laayoune**

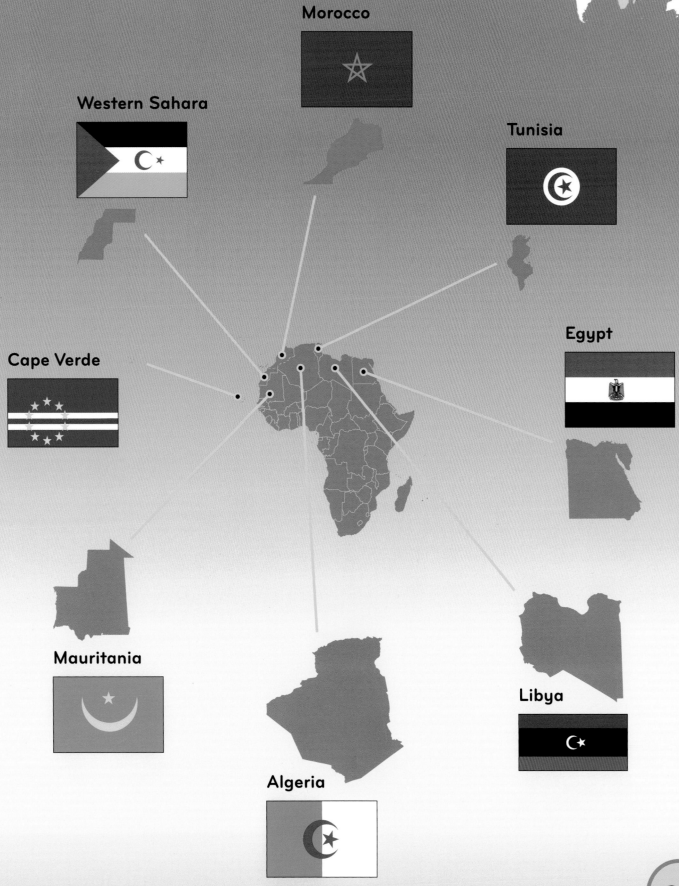

Morocco

Western Sahara

Tunisia

Egypt

Cape Verde

Mauritania

Libya

Algeria

Africa

Traditional African boats,
Senegal

Capital cities

Côte d'Ivoire (Ivory Coast)	**Yamoussoukro**
Guinea	**Conakry**
Guinea-Bissau	**Bissau**
Liberia	**Monrovia**
Mali	**Bamako**
Senegal	**Dakar**
Sierra Leone	**Freetown**
The Gambia	**Banjul**

Senegal

The Gambia

Mali

Guinea-Bissau

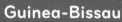

Côte d'Ivoire (Ivory Coast)

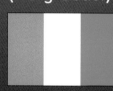

Guinea

Liberia

Sierra Leone

Africa

Capital cities

Benin	Porto-Novo
Burkina Faso	Ouagadougou
Chad	Ndjamena
Ghana	Accra
Niger	Niamey
Nigeria	Abuja
Togo	Lomé

Old rusted cannon in
Elmina Castle, Ghana

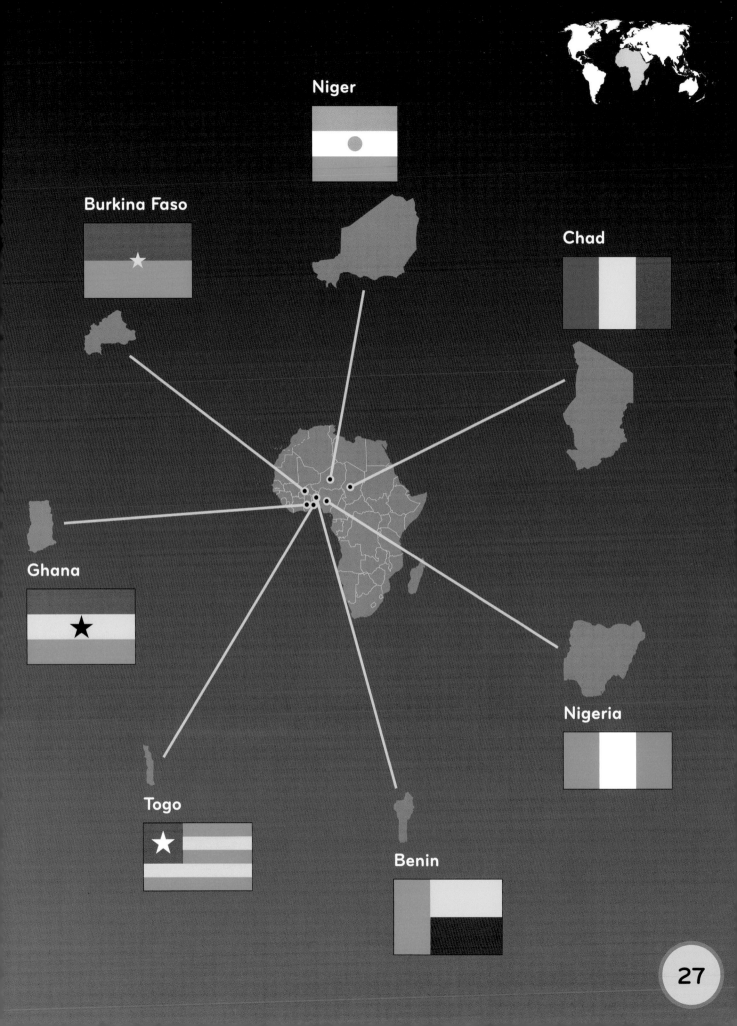

Niger

Burkina Faso

Chad

Ghana

Togo

Benin

Nigeria

27

Africa

Capital cities

Djibouti	Djibouti
Eritrea	Asmara
Ethiopia	Addis Ababa
Kenya	Nairobi
Somalia	Mogadishu
South Sudan	Juba
Sudan	Khartoum
Uganda	Kampala

Hot-air balloon over the Masai Mara, Kenya

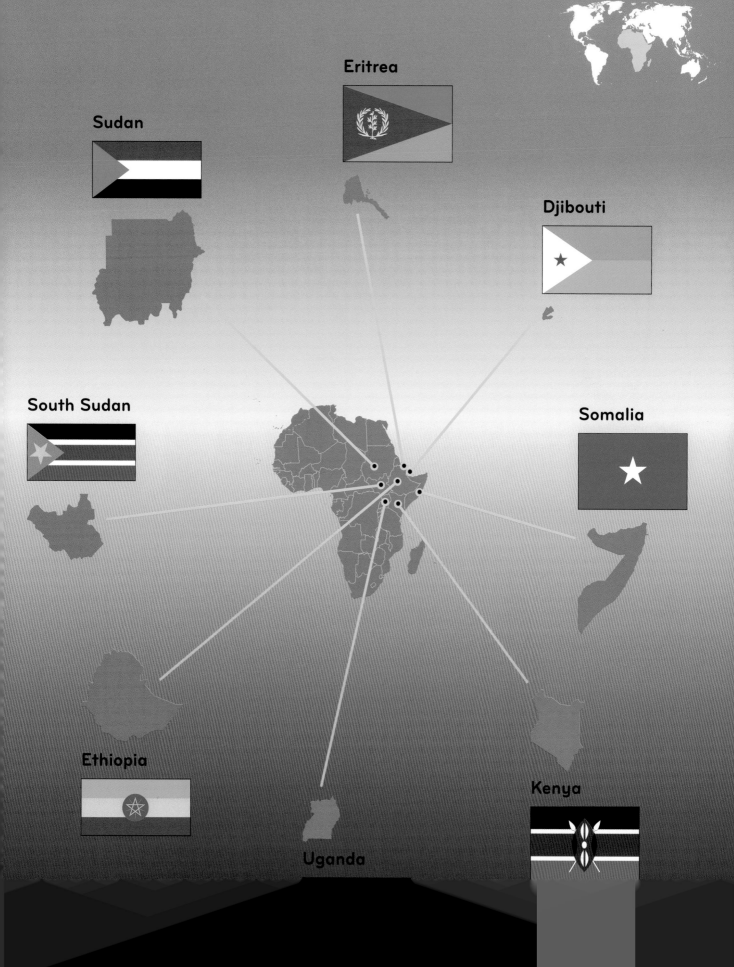

Sudan

Eritrea

Djibouti

South Sudan

Somalia

Ethiopia

Uganda

Kenya

Africa

African women praying,
Cameroon

Capital cities

Cameroon	Yaoundé
Central African Republic	Bangui
Equatorial Guinea	Malabo
Gabon	Libreville
St Helena, Ascension and Tristan da Cunha (UK)	Jamestown
São Tomé and Príncipe	São Tomé

Cameroon

Central African Republic

Equatorial Guinea

Gabon

St Helena, Ascension and Tristan da Cunha (UK)

São Tomé and Príncipe

Africa

Capital cities

Angola	**Luanda**
Burundi	**Bujumbura**
Congo	**Brazzaville**
Democratic Republic of the Congo	**Kinshasa**
Rwanda	**Kigali**
Tanzania	**Dodoma**
Zambia	**Lusaka**

Silverback gorilla,
Democratic Republic of the Congo

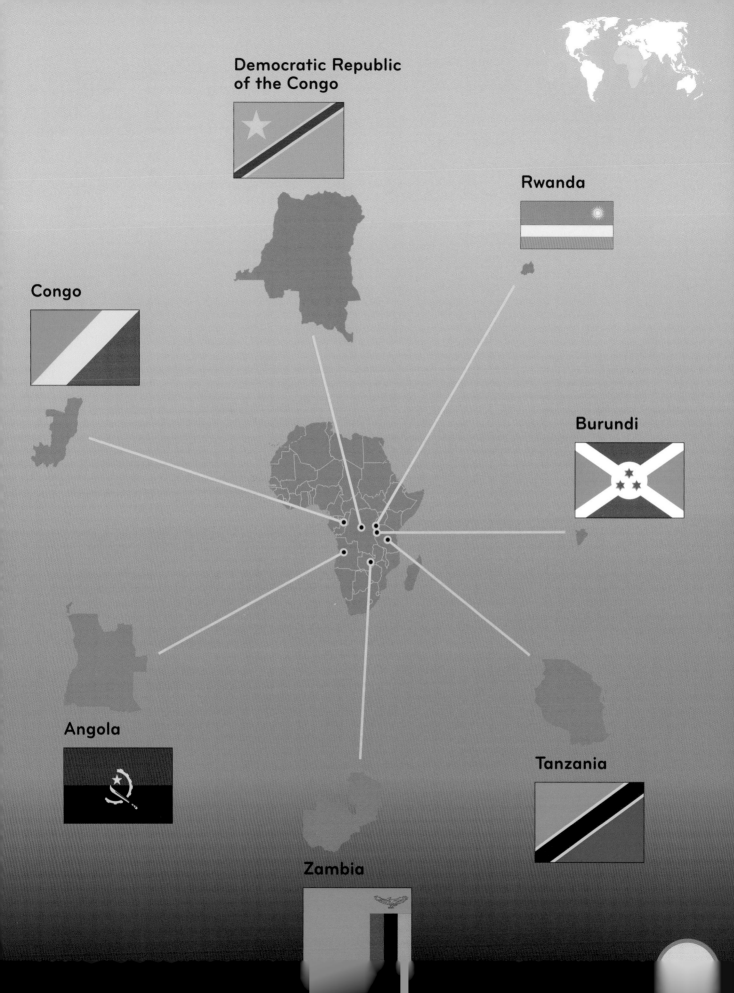

Democratic Republic
of the Congo

Rwanda

Congo

Burundi

Angola

Tanzania

Zambia

Africa

Capital cities

Botswana	**Gaborone**
Malawi	**Lilongwe**
Mozambique	**Maputo**
Namibia	**Windhoek**
Swaziland	**Mbabane**
Zimbabwe	**Harare**

Lioness with young lion cubs, Kalahari Desert, Botswana

Malawi

Zimbabwe

Mozambique

Namibia

Swaziland

Botswana

Africa

Capital cities

Comoros	**Moroni**
Lesotho	**Maseru**
Madagascar	**Antananarivo**
Mauritius	**Port Louis**
Mayotte (France)	**Dzaoudzi**
Réunion (France)	**St-Denis**
Seychelles	**Victoria**
South Africa	**Pretoria / Cape Town**

Springbok,
South Africa

Mayotte (France)

Seychelles

Comoros

Madagascar

South Africa

Mauritius

Lesotho

Réunion (France)

Asia

Uzbekistan

Georgia

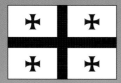

Armenia

Azerbaijan

Turkmenistan

Offshore rigs in the Caspian Sea,
Baku, Azerbaijan

Capital cities

Armenia	Yerevan
Azerbaijan	Baku
Georgia	T'bilisi
Turkmenistan	Ashgabat
Uzbekistan	Tashkent

Asia

Syria

Lebanon

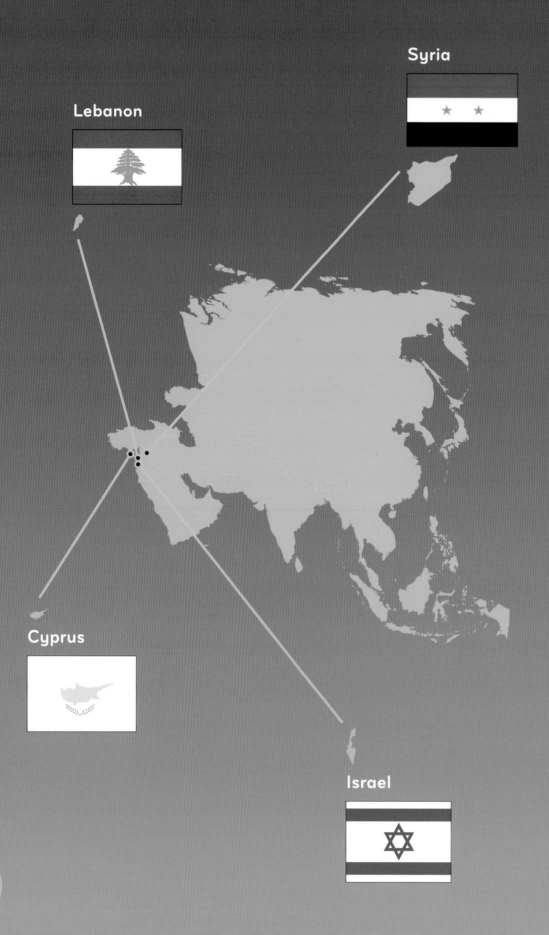

Cyprus

Israel

The Temple Mount,
Jerusalem, Israel

Capital cities

Cyprus	**Nicosia**
Israel	**Jerusalem***
Lebanon	**Beirut**
Syria	**Damascus**

*not internationally recognised

Asia

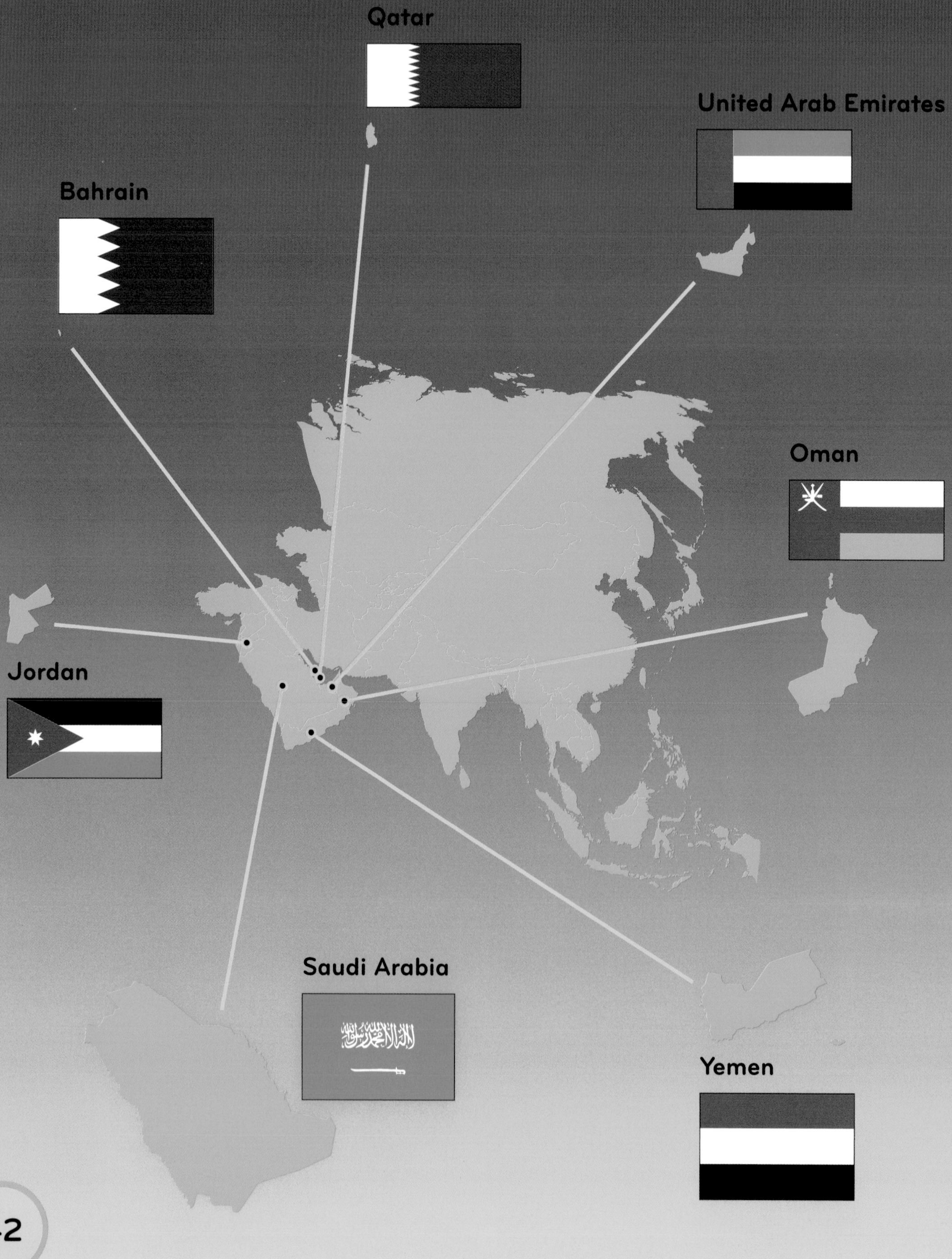

Qatar

United Arab Emirates

Bahrain

Oman

Jordan

Saudi Arabia

Yemen

Capital cities

Bahrain	Manama
Jordan	Amman
Oman	Muscat
Qatar	Doha
Saudi Arabia	Riyadh
United Arab Emirates	Abu Dhabi
Yemen	San'a

Camels in the desert,
Saudi Arabia

Asia

Iran

Iraq

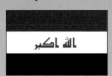

Afghanistan

Kuwait

Bangladesh

Pakistan

India

Taj Mahal, India

Capital cities

Afghanistan	Kabul
Bangladesh	Dhaka
India	New Delhi
Iran	Tehran
Iraq	Baghdad
Kuwait	Kuwait
Pakistan	Islamabad

Asia

Mongolia

China

Bhutan

Kazakhstan

Nepal

Tajikistan

Kyrgyzstan

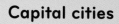

Capital cities

Bhutan	**Thimphu**
China	**Beijing**
Kazakhstan	**Astana**
Kyrgyzstan	**Bishkek**
Mongolia	**Ulan Bator**
Nepal	**Kathmandu**
Tajikistan	**Dushanbe**

Giant panda, China

Asia

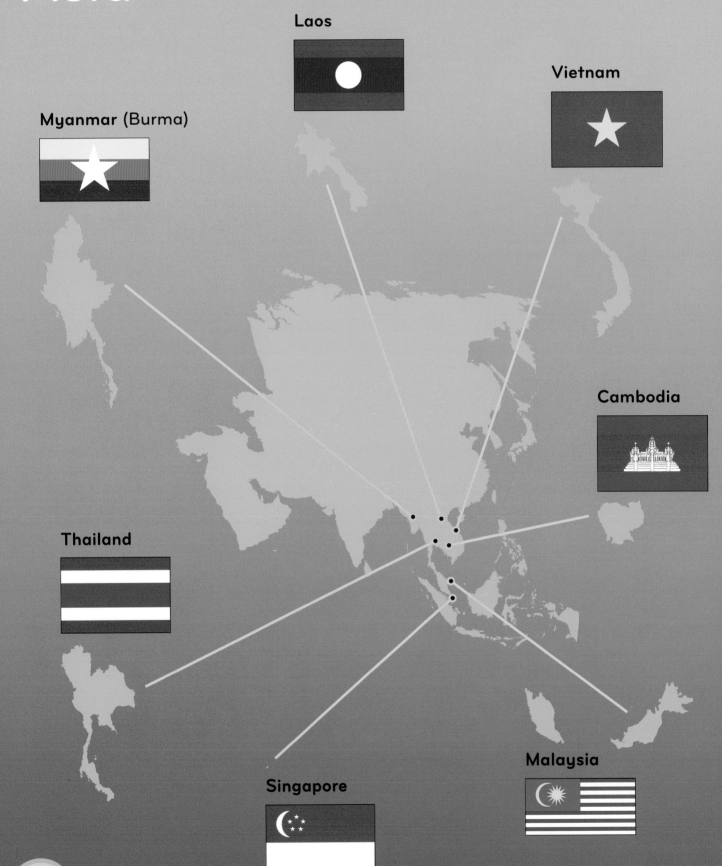

Laos

Vietnam

Myanmar (Burma)

Cambodia

Thailand

Malaysia

Singapore

Capital cities

Cambodia	**Phnom Penh**
Laos	**Vientiane**
Malaysia	**Kuala Lumpur / Putrajaya**
Myanmar (Burma)	
	Nay Pyi Taw / Yangon
Singapore	**Singapore**
Thailand	**Bangkok**
Vietnam	**Hanoi**

Orang-utan and her baby,
Borneo, Malaysia

Asia

North Korea

Japan

South Korea

Philippines

Palau

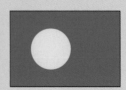

Capital cities

Japan	**Tokyo**
North Korea	**Pyongyang**
Palau	**Melekeok**
Philippines	**Manila**
South Korea	**Seoul**

Tarsier, Philippines

Asia

Sri Lanka

Maldives

Brunei

Indonesia

East Timor

Mosque,
Bandar Seri Begawan, Brunei

Capital cities

Brunei	Bandar Seri Begawan
East Timor	Dili
Indonesia	Jakarta
Maldives	Male
Sri Lanka	Sri Jayewardenepura Kotte

Grand Canyon, Arizona,
United States of America

Capital cities

Bermuda (UK)	Hamilton
Canada	Ottawa
Greenland (Denmark)	Nuuk
St Pierre and Miquelon (France)	St-Pierre
United States of America	Washington D.C.

Canada

Greenland (Denmark)

St Pierre and Miquelon (France)

Bermuda (UK)

United States of America

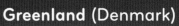

North America

Caribbean cruise ship,
Curaçao

Capital cities

Aruba (Netherlands)	Oranjestad
Cayman Islands (UK)	George Town
Cuba	Havana
Curaçao (Netherlands)	Willemstad
Dominican Republic	Santo Domingo
Haiti	Port-au-Prince
Jamaica	Kingston
Puerto Rico (USA)	San Juan
The Bahamas	Nassau
Turks and Caicos Islands (UK)	Grand Turk

Cuba

The Bahamas

Turks and Caicos Islands (UK)

Cayman Islands (UK)

Puerto Rico (USA)

Jamaica

Haiti

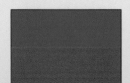

Dominican Republic

Aruba (Netherlands)

Curaçao (Netherlands)

North America

Capital cities

Anguilla (UK)	The Valley
Antigua and Barbuda	St John's
Barbados	Bridgetown
Dominica	Roseau
Grenada	St George's
Guadeloupe (France)	Basse-Terre
Martinique (France)	Fort-de-France
Montserrat (UK)	Brades
St Kitts and Nevis	Basseterre
St Lucia	Castries
St Vincent and the Grenadines	Kingstown
Trinidad and Tobago	Port of Spain
Virgin Islands (UK)	Road Town
Virgin Islands (USA)	Charlotte Amalie

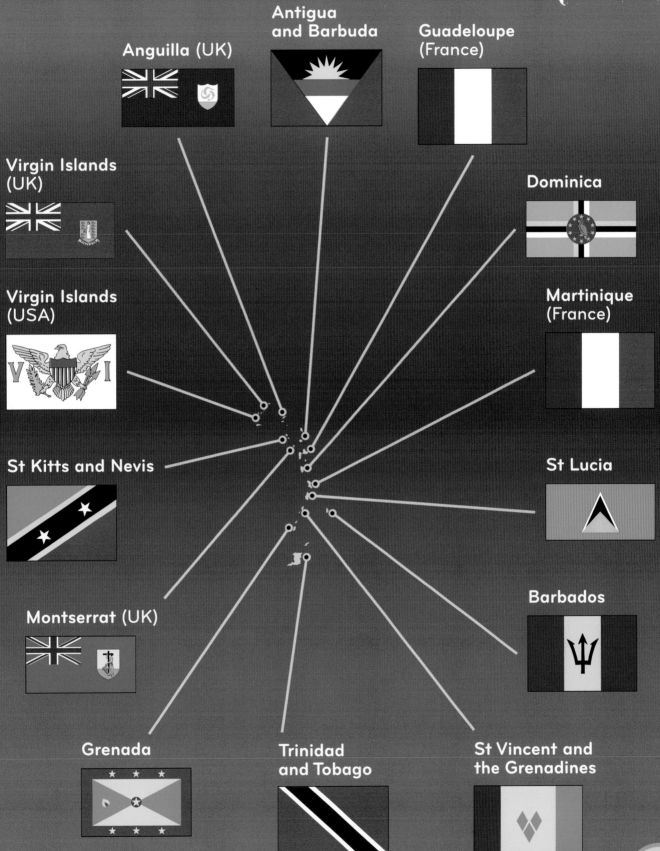

Anguilla (UK)

Antigua
and Barbuda

Guadeloupe
(France)

Virgin Islands
(UK)

Dominica

Virgin Islands
(USA)

Martinique
(France)

St Kitts and Nevis

St Lucia

Montserrat (UK)

Barbados

Grenada

Trinidad
and Tobago

St Vincent and
the Grenadines

North America

Capital cities

Belize	Belmopan
Costa Rica	San José
El Salvador	San Salvador
Guatemala	Guatemala City
Honduras	Tegucigalpa
Mexico	Mexico City
Nicaragua	Managua
Panama	Panama City

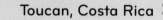

Toucan, Costa Rica

Mexico

Belize

Honduras

Guatemala

Nicaragua

El Salvador

Panama

Costa Rica

South America

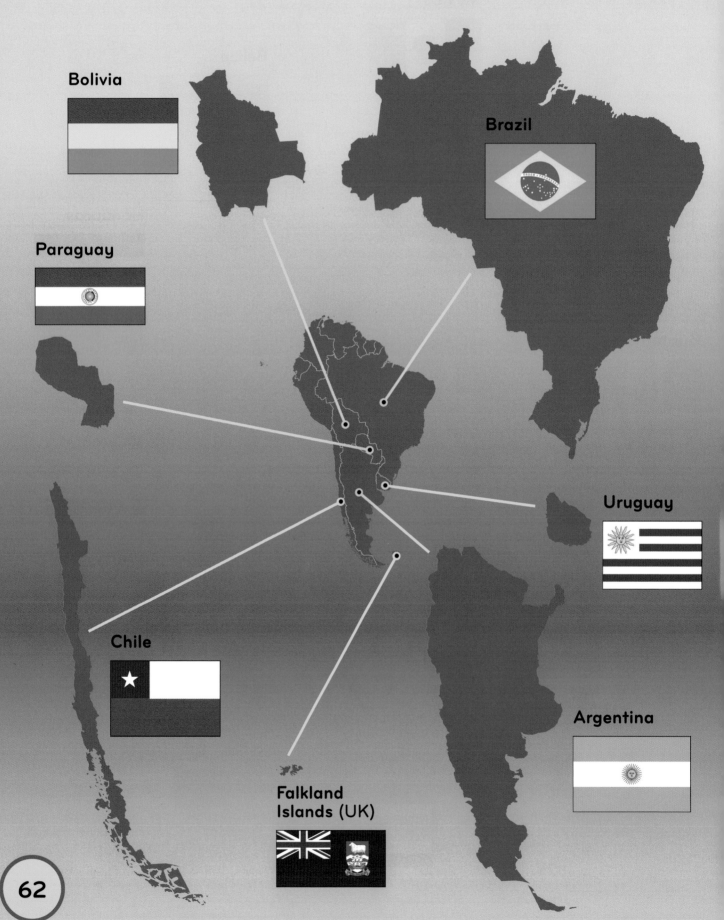

Bolivia

Paraguay

Brazil

Uruguay

Chile

Argentina

Falkland
Islands (UK)

Capital cities

Argentina	**Buenos Aires**
Bolivia	**La Paz / Sucre**
Brazil	**Brasília**
Chile	**Santiago**
Falkland Islands (UK)	**Stanley**
Paraguay	**Asunción**
Uruguay	**Montevideo**

Glacier in Patagonia,
Argentina

South America

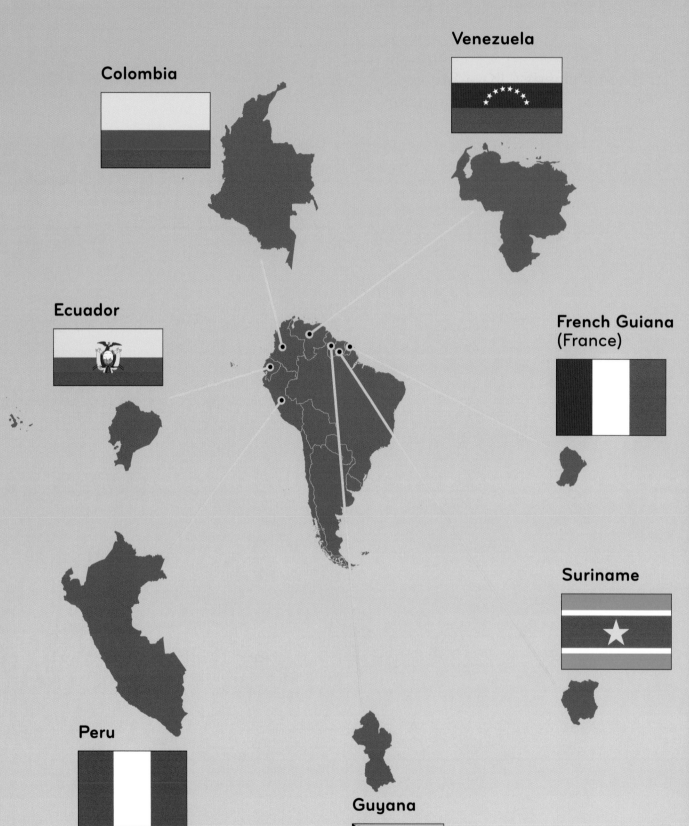

Colombia

Venezuela

Ecuador

French Guiana (France)

Suriname

Peru

Guyana

Capital cities

Colombia	**Bogotá**
Ecuador	**Quito**
French Guiana (France)	**Cayenne**
Guyana	**Georgetown**
Peru	**Lima**
Suriname	**Paramaribo**
Venezuela	**Caracas**

Machu Picchu, Peru

Oceania

Capital cities

Australia	Canberra
New Zealand	Wellington
Papua New Guinea	Port Moresby

Sydney Opera House,
Sydney, Australia

Papua New Guinea

Australia

New Zealand

Oceania

Capital cities

Federated States of Micronesia	**Palikir**
Marshall Islands	**Delap-Uliga-Djarrit**
Nauru	**Yaren**
Solomon Islands	**Honiara**

Rainbow lorikeets,
Solomon Islands

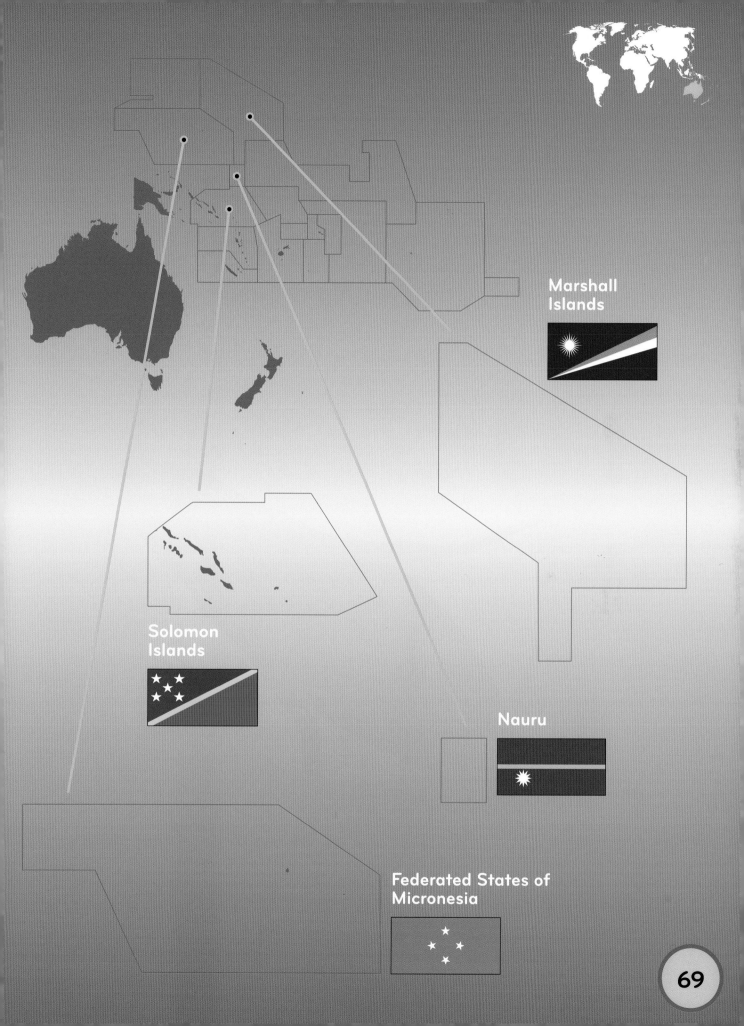

Marshall
Islands

Solomon
Islands

Nauru

Federated States of
Micronesia

Oceania

Capital cities

Fiji	Suva
New Caledonia (France)	Nouméa
Tuvalu	Vaiaku
Vanuatu	Port Vila

Fishing, Fiji

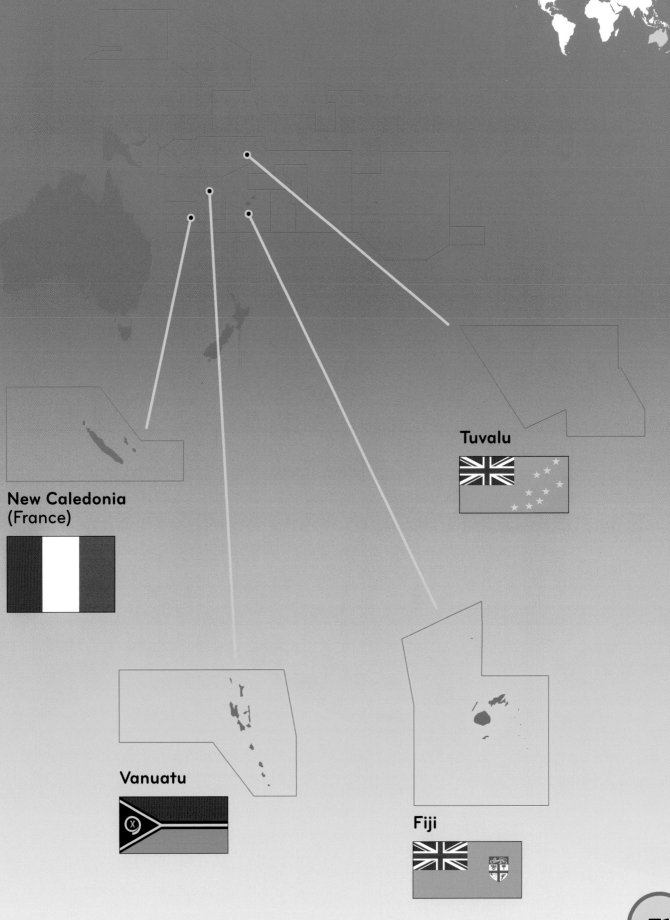

New Caledonia
(France)

Vanuatu

Tuvalu

Fiji

Oceania

Capital cities

American Samoa (USA)	**Fagatogo**
Cook Islands (New Zealand)	
	Avarua
Kiribati	Bairiki
Samoa	Apia
Tonga	Nuku'alofa

Shell fans, Cook Islands

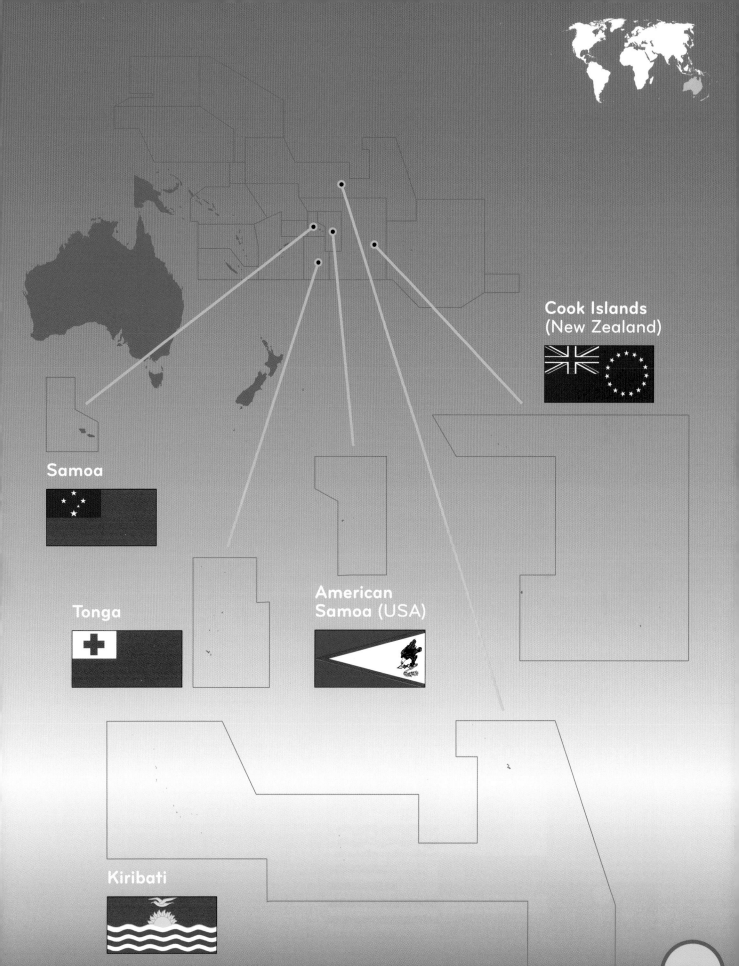

Cook Islands
(New Zealand)

Samoa

Tonga

American
Samoa (USA)

Kiribati

Types of Flags

Flags with animals

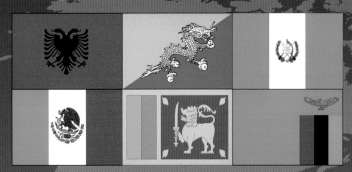

Flags featuring a star or stars

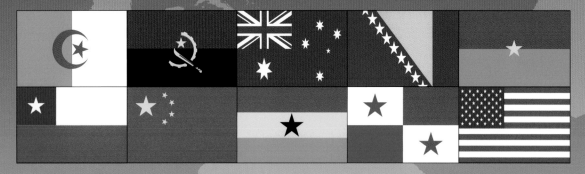

Flags featuring a sun

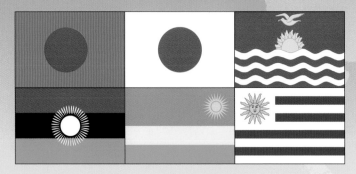

Flags with a moon

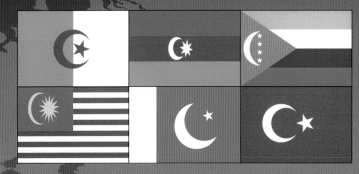

Flags with triangles

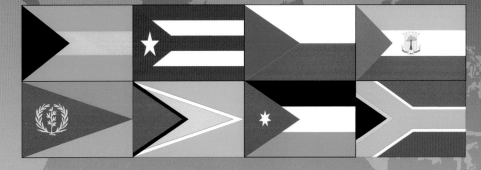

Striped flags

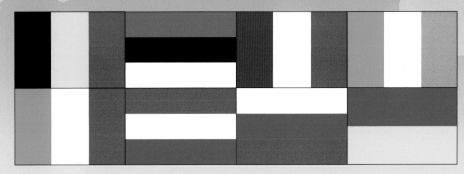

Quiz

Whose flag is this?

There are 20 country flags and 20 country names shown below.
Match up the country names to their flag.

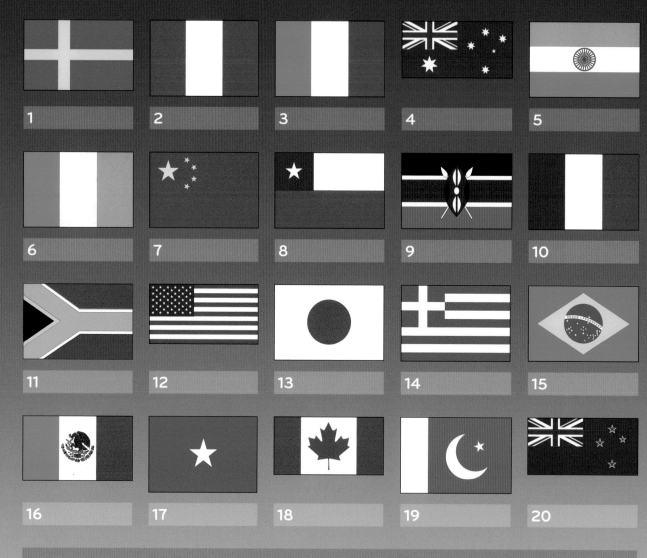

1	2	3	4	5
6	7	8	9	10
11	12	13	14	15
16	17	18	19	20

Japan	Canada	Sweden	Kenya	Chile
Greece	Australia	USA	South Africa	Brazil
Somalia	Pakistan	France	Ireland	Peru
India	New Zealand	China	Mexico	Italy

Spot the difference!

Look at the pairs of flags below. Guess the country each belongs to and find the difference between each pair.

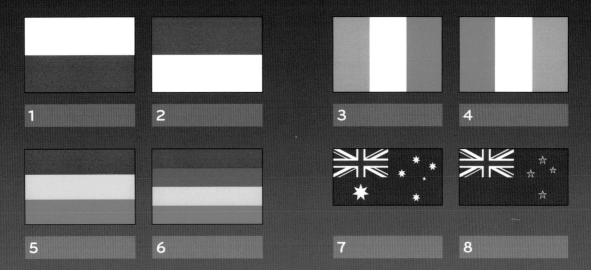

Match the country to its flag

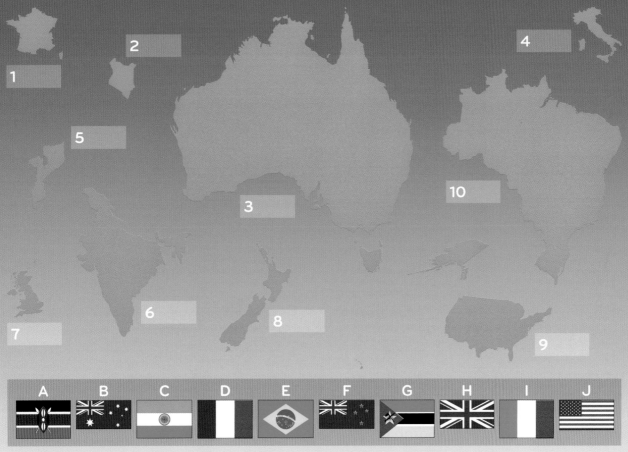

Answers at the back of the book

Index

Lithuania	10	Peru	64	Tajikistan	46
Luxembourg	12	Philippines	50	Tanzania	33
Macedonia	18	Poland	14	Thailand	48
Madagascar	37	Portugal	6	Togo	27
Malawi	35	Puerto Rico (USA)	57	Tonga	73
Malaysia	48	Qatar	42	Trinidad and Tobago	59
Maldives	52	Réunion (France)	37	Tristan da Cunha (UK)	31
Mali	25	Romania	20	Tunisia	23
Malta	16	Russian Federation	20	Turkey	18
Marshall Islands	69	Rwanda	33	Turkmenistan	38
Martinique (France)	59	St Helena (UK)	31	Turks and Caicos Islands	
Mauritania	23	St Kitts and Nevis	59	(UK)	57
Mauritius	37	St Lucia	59	Tuvalu	71
Mayotte (France)	37	St Pierre and Miquelon		Uganda	29
Mexico	61	(France)	55	Ukraine	20
Moldova	20	St Vincent and the		United Arab Emirates	42
Monaco	6	Grenadines	59	United Kingdom	8
Mongolia	46	Samoa	73	United States of	
Montenegro	18	San Marino	16	America	55
Montserrat (UK)	59	São Tomé and Príncipe	31	Uruguay	62
Morocco	23	Saudi Arabia	42	Uzbekistan	38
Mozambique	35	Senegal	25	Vanuatu	71
Myanmar (Burma)	48	Serbia	16	Vatican City	16
Namibia	35	Seychelles	37	Venezuela	64
Nauru	69	Sierra Leone	25	Vietnam	48
Nepal	46	Singapore	48	Virgin Islands (UK)	59
Netherlands	12	Slovakia	14	Virgin Islands (USA)	59
New Caledonia		Slovenia	14	Western Sahara	23
(France)	71	Solomon Islands	69	Yemen	42
New Zealand	67	Somalia	29	Zambia	33
Nicaragua	61	South Africa	37	Zimbabwe	35
Niger	27	South Korea	50		
Nigeria	27	South Sudan	29		
North Korea	50	Spain	6		
Norway	10	Sri Lanka	52		
Oman	42	Sudan	29		
Pakistan	44	Suriname	64		
Palau	50	Swaziland	35		
Panama	61	Sweden	10		
Papua New Guinea	67	Switzerland	12		
Paraguay	62	Syria	40		

Quiz answers

Quiz 1 (page 76)

Whose flag is this?

1 Sweden	2 Peru	3 Italy	4 Australia	5 India
6 Ireland	7 China	8 Chile	9 Kenya	10 France
11 South Africa	12 USA	13 Japan	14 Greece	15 Brazil
16 Mexico	17 Somalia	18 Canada	19 Pakistan	20 New Zealand

Quiz 2 (page 77)

Spot the difference!
1. Poland flag has red stripe at the bottom of the flag 2. Indonesia has red stripe at the top.
3. Cote d'Ivoire and 4. Ireland have stripes in a different order.
5. Bolivia and 6. Mauritius have a different number of stripes.
7. Australia flag has white stars 8. New Zealand has red stars.

Quiz 3 (page 77)

Match the country to its flag

1 France D		2 Kenya A
3 Australia B		4 Italy I
5 Mozambique G		6 India C
7 UK H		8 New Zealand F
9 USA J		10 Brazil E

Image credits